KU-482-430

Easter Vigil
and other poems

WITHDRAWN FROM STOCK

COMHAIRLE CHONTAE ÁTHA CLIATH THEAS
SOUTH DUBLIN COUNTY LIBRARIES

SOUTH DUBLIN BOOKSTORE
TO RENEW ANY ITEM TEL: 459 7834

Items should be returned on or before the last date below. Fines,
as displayed in the Library, will be charged on overdue items.

EASTER VIGIL

and other poems

Karol Wojtyla

TOTUS TUUS

Translated by Jerzy Peterkiewicz

HUTCHINSON OF LONDON

CO. DUBLIN
LIBRARY SERVICE
Acc No. 463,330ᴬ
Class No. 821/HOJ
891.85/WOJ
Cated. Classed
Prepared
Re-Bound £2.95
INVOICE No. 40892

Hutchinson & Co. (Publishers) Ltd
3 Fitzroy Square, London W1P 6JD

London Melbourne Sydney Auckland
Wellington Johannesburg and agencies
throughout the world

English translation first published 1979

© Libreria Editrice Vaticana, Vatican City, 1979
Translation © Jerzy Peterkiewicz 1979

Set in VIP Bembo by D.P. Media Ltd, Hitchin, Herts

Printed in Great Britain by Wm Clowes and Sons Ltd, Beccles

ISBN 0 09 138800 7

Frontispiece: *James Andanson / Sygma / John Hillelson Agency*

Contents

Acknowledgements

Authorization to translate these poems from the Polish original was graciously granted by the author.

I wish to express my gratitude to the following people who have helped in various ways: Dr B. Andrzejewski, Rosamond Batchelor, Catharine Carver, Janina Lubaś Cunnelly, Dr L. Kukulski, Father J. Mirewicz, S.J., Mr J. Turowicz, editor of *Tygodnik Powszechny*, Mr J. Woźniakowski, former editor of *Znak*, and the Polish Library in London.

My very special thanks are offered to Carol O'Brien of Hutchinson for her encouragement and advice during the preparation of this book.

Introduction

When Cardinal Wojtyla was elected Pope in October 1978 it became known that he had published poetry under an assumed name. This item of news surprised people even in Poland, for the identity of 'Andrzej Jawien', the pen-name he used for sixteen years, was a well-guarded secret among his close friends. Between 1950 and 1966 poems signed by Jawien were appearing in two Catholic periodicals, *The Universal Weekly* and *The Sign*, both published in Cracow where Karol Wojtyla rose to prominence, first as Bishop (at thirty-eight the youngest in the country) and then as Cardinal, from 1967 to his election to the throne of Peter.

That he wrote verse in his early years is not surprising. Poles are a language-conscious people; they have an old and sophisticated literature in which poetry plays a dominant part. They genuinely appreciate verse and know much of it by heart. Wojtyla was no exception. A year before the outbreak of the Second World War he enrolled in the University of Cracow to study Polish literature – not theology. The priest's vocation came later during the hard years of the German occupation when he had to support himself as a worker in the quarries and in a chemical factory. But his passionate interest in poetry remained: in Cracow he joined a clandestine 'Rhapsodic Theatre' which developed a new form of dramatic expression to be continued by others once the German occupation was over.

In November 1946, however, at the age of twenty-six, Wojtyla was consecrated priest. A few years later 'Jawien' appears as his companion on the difficult road to self-knowledge. Two vocations ran parallel in his life: the priest's which was open and the poet's which was concealed if not secret. The pseudonym itself is an interesting choice. Jawien is a character from a modern Polish novel which must have impressed Wojtyla at the time. To a native speaker the root of the name suggests someone realizing himself, coming to light. And Jawien did come to light after 16

October 1978: the author of the Polish poems was now Pope John Paul II.

The texts selected for this book are representative in style and subject matter. But, above all, they indicate different stages in the spiritual growth of the future Pope. The dates of their publication point to dramatic changes in him and in the world around him, from 1950 (when he was a young curate and a research student) to 1962, the year of the Second Vatican Council which he attended as Bishop, and finally 1966 when the millennium of Christianity in Poland was celebrated, and he wrote his 'Easter Vigil 1966'. A year later he became Cardinal.

The first poems belong to a cruel decade for the Church in Eastern Europe. In the early 1950s the communist rulers launched a big offensive against religious faith on all fronts: in education, the press, radio, publishing and, of course, in areas directly affecting the work of the clergy, from parish priest to bishop. The Primate of Poland was kept prisoner in a cloister. Doing good in those circumstances meant working in silent heroism towards 'difficult good', to use a phrase from one of Wojtyla's later poems. The dark night of the spirit was then not only the mystical concept of St John of the Cross to be contemplated by the pious: it became a frightening reality for every Christian.

One has to remember that anything which is printed in Poland is subject to censorship. Although Wojtyla's poems are not overtly political, they too had to pass the censor's eye. A poem like 'Simon of Cyrene' means something quite different if we bear this in mind when reading it: the Cyrenean who helped Christ to carry the cross is also a man of our time.

In 1956 Wojtyla wrote a startling and difficult poem, 'The Quarry'. It was a crucial year in the relations between the Church and the communist government in post-war Poland. The Primate was released after his long imprisonment. The philosophic

10

argument in 'The Quarry' is about work, anger and love. The language moves from physical detail, almost tangible in its concreteness, to thought reflecting thought. Wojtyla probes into emotions that are born from man's struggle with matter. Energy passes from hand to stone, the stone yields its strength; anger and love are in the balance. The poem ends with a moving elegy in memory of a fellow-worker who was killed in an accident. 'They took his body and walked in a silent line'; the body is laid on 'a sheet of gravel' – a sombre recollection of his own experiences when he worked in the quarries near Cracow.

Work is a theme that runs through Wojtyla's poems. There are sharply drawn 'profiles' in the Cyrenean cycle: a car factory worker, a worker from an armaments factory, a woman typing eight hours a day (black letters hang from reddened eyelids), a man of intellect, an actor, a girl disappointed in love. Ordinary detail is here transformed by an understanding eye. Like the hand, the eye is constantly present in Wojtyla's reality; so are thought, space and the heart. He is a philosopher poet who sees God's mystery in a paradox and also in a simple picture registered by the eye. Wojtyla's intellectual abilities were recognized early: he taught social ethics in the Cracow seminary and for a few years was Professor of Ethics in the Catholic University at Lublin.

He was consecrated Bishop in 1958, a year after the publication of 'The Quarry'. He became a public man, and the poet's vocation had to be veiled even more. A group of short poems written in Rome during the Second Vatican Council (autumn 1962) appeared in print simply under the initials *A.J.* So did 'Easter Vigil 1966'. No more Andrzej Jawien. Wojtyla was always self-effacing and reticent about his poetic work – his friends from Cracow confirm this. So Jawien's poems were never collected in a volume. Only one Polish anthology, devoted to Marian poetry, includes sections from his cycle 'Mother'.

The Roman sequence of 1962 ('The Church') is meditative but the voice that speaks in poems like 'Marble floor' or 'The crypt' has singular authority. The lines now seem almost prophetic, inspired by the great basilica from which he was to emerge as Peter's successor sixteen years later. It is not yet time to consider the artistic merits of Wojtyla's texts as a whole. His language is often charged with unusual metaphors and his way of describing physical detail is reminiscent of Hopkins's *inscape*. The sensitivity comes from a child's astonishment, intensified in his case by early deprivation: Wojtyla lost his mother at the age of nine.

This selection begins with poems in honour of the Virgin Mary to whom the present Pope has deep devotion, as does the country where he was born. The very first Polish poem, written in the thirteenth century, is a hymn to the Mother of God. This book ends with poems on man and history written in 1966, the year when Poland celebrated its thousand years as a Christian state.

Some literary comparisons have to be made, however briefly. Wojtyla came to know the blazing intellect of St John of the Cross, the Spanish mystic, when he wrote a doctoral thesis on the problems of faith in his works. St John shows how to express truth through paradox and negation (to know without knowing, to die in not dying). Another obvious inspiration was a Pole, Cyprian Norwid (1821–83) whose poetry and ideas had a profound influence on Wojtyla's generation. For Norwid, to understand the meaning of work was essential for the interpretation of all creative acts; he saw beauty as 'God's profile': the Creator cannot be seen face to face. In English literature Gerard Manley Hopkins is a striking parallel. As a Jesuit priest he was always prepared to abandon his writing should his religious life demand such a sacrifice.

This poses a final problem. Is the poet–priest more vulnerable than other poets because of his dual vocation? We find a significant comment in Cardinal Wojtyla's preface to an anthol-

12

ogy of poems written by priests. He asks how 'the two vocations, the priest's and the poet's, co-exist and act on each other in
the same person'. Such a question, he adds, touches on the
personal secret which each poet carries in him; and is this secret
not revealed in his writing?

I believe that the poems in this book provide a subtle key to the
rich personality of Pope John Paul II. This is poetry of thought,
sometimes difficult, yet always ready for dialogue with another
mind. And the heart that inspires the thought beats with com-
passion for Simon the Cyrenean, Mary Magdalene and the
Samaritan woman, in whose shadows we still live.

Jerzy Peterkiewicz

Note on translation

Polish verse is essentially syllabic whereas English is stressed. In
Karol Wojtyla's poems, lines are often long – sixteen or even
twenty syllables – when compared with the standard thirteen-
syllable line. In translation some of the long lines have been
divided in order to help the clarity of argument, especially in
complex poems like 'The Quarry'.

Assonance rather than rhyme characterizes the texts in the original and stanza patterns are loose. I have tried to convey those
metaphors, juxtapositions of thought and even idiosyncratic
turns of phrase which mark the author's individual manner. It is
the mind behind the text that one wants to bring closer to the
reader. His participation is what a translator hopes for, at the end
of his labours.

J.P.

from Mother

Her amazement at her only child

Light piercing, gradually, everyday events;
a woman's eyes, hands
used to them since childhood.
Then brightness flared, too huge for simple days,
and hands clasped when the words lost their space.

In that little town, my son, where they knew us together,
you called me mother; but no one had eyes to see
the astounding events as they took place day by day.
Your life became the life of the poor
in your wish to be with them through the work of your hands.

I knew: the light that lingered in ordinary things,
like a spark sheltered under the skin of our days –
the light was you;
it did not come from me.

And I had more of you in that luminous silence
than I had of you as the fruit of my body, my blood.

15

John beseeches her

Don't lower the wave of my heart,
it swells to your eyes, Mother;
don't alter love, but bring the wave to me
in your translucent hands.

He asked for this.

I am John the fisherman. There isn't much
in me to love.

I feel I am still on that lake shore,
gravel crunching under my feet –
and, suddenly – Him.

You will embrace His mystery in me no more,
yet quietly I spread round your thoughts like myrtle.
And calling you Mother – His wish –
I beseech you: may this word
never grow less for you.

True, it's not easy to measure the meaning
of the words He breathed into us both
so that all earlier love in those words
should be concealed.

Embraced by new time

My depths are seen into, I am seen through and through.
Open to sight I rise, in that vision gently submerge.
For a long time nobody knew of this;
I told no one the expression of your eyes.

How attentive your stillness: it will always be part of me.
I lift myself towards it, will one day grow so used to it
that I will stand still, transparent as water vanishing
into a dry river-bed – though my body will remain.
Your disciples will come, and hear that my heart-beat has
    stopped.

My life will no longer be weighed deep in my blood,
the road will no longer slip away from my weary feet.
New time now shines in my fading eyes:
it will consume me, and dwell with my heart.
And all shall be full at the last, and left for thought's delight.

I will open out my song and know its smallest sound,
I will open out my song intent on the whole of your life,
my song possessed by the Event so simple and clear,
which begins in every man, visibly there, yet secret.

In me it was made flesh, was revealed in song with grace,
and came to many, and in them found its own space.

from Song of the Brightness of Water

'Jesus answered and said to her: Whosoever drinketh of this water shall thirst again; but he that shall drink of the water that I will give him shall not thirst for ever.'
JOHN 4 : 13

Looking into the well at Sichar

Look now at the silver scales in the water
where the depth trembles
like the retina of an eye recording an image.

With the broad leaves' reflection
touching your face
water washes tiredness round your eyes.

Still far from the spring.

Tired eyes are the sign
that the night's dark waters
flow through words into prayer.

(Consider how arid, how arid our souls.)

The light from the well pulsates with tears:
a gust of dreams,
passers-by think, brought them down.

The well sparkles with leaves that leap
to your eyes. Reflected green
glints round your face
in the shimmering depth.

How far to the spring?

Multitudes tremble in you, transfixed
by the light of your words
as eyes by the brightness of water.

You know them in weariness. You know them in light.

Words spoken by the woman at the well, on departing

From this moment my ignorance
closes behind me like the door
through which you entered, recognizing
all I do not know.
And through me you led many people in silence,
many roads, and the turmoil of the streets.

The Samaritan woman

It joined us together, the well;
the well led me into you.
No one between us but light
deep in the well, the pupil of the eye
set in an orbit of stones.

Within your eyes, I,
drawn by the well,
am enclosed.

The Samaritan woman meditates

I – yes I – conscious then of my awakening
as a man in a stream, aware of his image,
is suddenly raised from the mirror and brought
to himself, holding his breath in amazement,
swaying over his light.

I was raised – how, I don't know. Yet conscious
then of myself, myself before,
now divided – only by waking?
The wall opens. I often passed through this wall
not knowing that it divided
me from myself.

Yes, I am raised. Everything seems as before:
the mules with their burdens
slithering down the hill.
The world goes up, falls down
into houses carried through deep blue air
(in vain, in vain).
Lamps light up again in the midst of awaited stars.

The burden inside that you took from me – I will sense
slowly, and measure with weariness
through seasons of struggle, trying to bring out
a small part of that simple harmony
you possess without strain
beyond measure.

Straining you planted
a particle in me. But this I know:
the inner burden you took away
is not hung in the void.
Scales will never tell its weight
or differentiate.
This undifferentiated state
I weigh and I am light again.
A flame rescued from dry wood
has no weight in its luminous flight
yet lifts the heavy lid of night.

Song of the brightness of water

From this depth – I came only to draw water
in a jug – so long ago, this brightness
still clings to my eyes – the perception I found,
and so much empty space, my own,
reflected in the well.

Yet it is good. I can never take all of you
into me. Stay then as a mirror in the well.
Leaves and flowers remain, and each astonished gaze
brings them down
to my eyes transfixed more by light
than by sorrow.

from Thought – Strange Space

Thought's resistance to words

Sometimes it happens in conversation: we stand
facing truth and lack the words,
have no gesture, no sign;
and yet – we feel – no word, no gesture
or sign would convey the whole image
that we must enter alone and face like Jacob.

This isn't mere wrestling with images
carried in our thoughts;
we fight with the likeness of all things
that inwardly constitute man.
But when we act can our deeds surrender
the ultimate truths we presume to ponder?

Words' resistance to thought

If he suffers, deprived of vision,
he must tear through the thicket of signs
to the word's very centre,
its weight the ripeness of fruit.

Is this the weight Jacob felt,
pressing him down
when tired stars sank within him,
the eyes of his flock?

Error

How to extract the still centre of thought?
I can bend the street to one side,
find fault in the eyes of girls, of boys
walking by;
and when the lines of cars converge
only their windscreens perhaps
capture infinity.

And people say:
our thought is bound up with the clarity of things,
our thought remains true to the power
of ordinary things.
But if still so few of them are open to us
surely our thought is not complete.

The Quarry

I. Material

1

Listen: the even knocking of hammers,
so much their own,
I project on to the people
to test the strength of each blow.
Listen now: electric current
cuts through a river of rock.
And a thought grows in me day after day:
the greatness of work is inside man.

Hard and cracked
his hand is differently charged
by the hammer
and thought differently unravels in stone
as human energy splits from the strength of stone
cutting the bloodstream, an artery
in the right place.

Look, how love feeds
on this well-grounded anger
which flows into people's breath
as a river bent by the wind,
and which is never spoken, but just breaks high vocal cords.

Passers-by scuttle off into doorways,
someone whispers: 'Yet here is a great force.'

Fear not. Man's daily deeds have a wide span,
a strait river-bed can't imprison them long.
Fear not. For centuries they all stand in Him,
and you look at Him now
through the even knocking of hammers.

2

Bound are the blocks of stone, the low-voltage wire
cuts deep in their flesh, an invisible whip –
stones know this violence.
When an elusive blast rips their ripe compactness
and tears them from their eternal simplicity,
the stones know this violence.
Yet can the current unbind their full strength?
It is he who carries that strength in his hands:
the worker.

3

Hands are the heart's landscape. They split sometimes
like ravines into which an undefined force rolls.
The very same hands which man only opens
when his palms have had their fill of toil.
Now he sees: because of him alone others can walk in peace.

Hands are a landscape. When they split, the pain of their sores
surges free as a stream.
But no thought of pain –
no grandeur in pain alone.
For his own grandeur he does not know how to name.

4

No, not just hands drooping with the hammer's weight,
not the taut torso, muscles shaping their own style,
but thought informing his work,
deep, knotted in wrinkles on his brow,
and over his head, joined in a sharp arc, shoulders and veins
    vaulted.

So for a moment he is a Gothic building
cut by a vertical thought born in the eyes.
No, not a profile alone,
not a mere figure between God and the stone,
sentenced to grandeur and error.

II. Inspiration

1

Work starts within, outside it takes such space
that it soon seizes hands, then the limits of breath.
Look – your will strikes a deep bell in stone,
thought strikes certainty, a peak
both for heart and for hand.

For this certainty of mind, this certainty of eye,
for this vertical line
you pay with a generous hand.
The stone yields you its strength,
and man matures through work
which inspires him to difficult good.

With work then it begins: the growing in the heart and the mind,
great events, a multitude of men are drawn in.
Listen to love that ripens in hammers, in even sounds.
Children will carry them into the future, singing:
'In our fathers' hearts
work knew no bounds.'

2

This inspiration will not end with hands.
Down to stone centres it descends through man's heart
and from the heart's centre the history of stones
grows large in the layers of earth.
And in man grows the equilibrium
which love learns through anger.

Neither is ever exhausted in man,
ever ceases in the shoulders' tension,
in the heart's hidden gesture.
They partake of each other, fulfilling each other,
raised by a lever which joins movement and thought
in an unbreakable circle.

If from afar you want to enter and stay in man
you must merge these two forces into a language
simple beyond words
(your speech must not break at the lever's tension:
the fulcrum of anger and love).
Then no one will ever tear You
out from the centre of man.

III. Participation

The light of this rough plank,
recently carved from a trunk,
is pouring the vastness
of work indivisible into your palms.
The taut hand rests on this Act
which permeates all things in man.

Man, his eyes tired, his eyebrows sharp,
and stones have edges sharp as knives.
Electric current cuts the walls,
an invisible whip. And the sun,
July sun: white fire in the stone.

My hands – do they belong to the light
that now cuts across the railway track,
the pickaxes, the fence overhead?
They belong to the heart and the heart doesn't swear
(keep heart from lips fouled by cursing).

How splendid these men, no airs, no graces;
I know you, look into your hearts,
no pretence stands between us.
Some hands are for toil, some for the cross.
The fence over your heads, pickaxes scattered on the tracks.

Beware of hollows in stone. Electric current
fells columns, pouring them like dust through a sieve.
The young look for a road. All roads
drive straight at my heart. Do stones forgive?

Let the world rest on this balance of hands.
Keep it unchanged in every explosion
of man and stone, over that fence
but a few steps away –
sometimes a child runs carelessly past.

This balance you hold all alone
is both too far and too near.
Now we stoop, now we climb
(the child is careless, might quickly run by).

There is silence again between heart, stone, and tree.
Whoever enters Him keeps his own self.
He who does not
has no full part in the business of this world
despite all appearances.

IV. (In memory of a fellow-worker)

1

He wasn't alone. His muscles grew into the flesh of the crowd,
energy their pulse, as long as they held a hammer,
as long as his feet felt the ground.
And a stone smashed his temples
and cut through his heart's chamber.

2

They took his body, and walked in a silent line.

3

Toil still lingered about him, a sense of wrong.
They wore grey blouses, boots ankle deep in mud.
In this they showed the end.

4

How violently his time halted: the pointers on the low-voltage
    dials
jerked, then dropped to zero again.
White stone now within him, eating into his being,
taking over enough of him to turn him into stone.

5

Who will lift up that stone, unfurl his thoughts again
under the cracked temples? So plaster cracks on the wall.
They laid him down, his back on a sheet of gravel.
His wife came, worn out with worry; his son returned from
    school.

6

Should his anger now flow into the anger of others?
It was maturing in him through its own truth and love.
Should he be used by those who come after,
deprived of substance, unique and deeply his own?

7

The stones on the move again: a wagon bruising the flowers.
Again the electric current cuts deep into the walls.
But the man has taken with him the world's inner structure,
where the greater the anger, the higher the explosion of love.

from Profiles of a Cyrenean

'And they forced one Simon, a Cyrenean, who passed by coming out of the
country, the father of Alexander and of Rufus, to take up his cross.'

MARK 15 : 21

Before I could discern many profiles

1

A profile among trees, different among pillars
and different again in the street, melting into its wet surface.
Different is the profile of a man standing at his own door;
different a victor's profile: a Greek demigod.

I know the Cyrenean's profile best,
from every conceivable point of view.
The profile always starts alongside the other Man;
it falls from his shoulders
to break off exactly where
that other Man is most himself,
least defenceless

(he would be defenceless if
what is in him and of him
did not form a vertical line, but gave way).

Life tells me unceasingly
about such a profile, about that other Man.
(Profile becomes cross-section.)

2

Feet search the grass. The earth.
Insects drill the greenery, swaying the stream of the sun.
Feet wear down cobbles, the cobbled street
wears down feet. No pathos. Thoughts in the crowd, unspoken.

Take a thought if you can – plant its root
in the artisans' hands, in the fingers
of women typing eight hours a day:
black letters hang from reddened eyelids.

Take a thought, make man complete,
or allow him to begin himself anew,
or let him just help You perhaps
and You lead him on.

3

Why is it not so, Magdalene, Simon of Cyrene?
Do you remember that first step which you are still
taking all the time?

4

Grass waving, a green hammock, a breezy cradle of bees.
Stone slabs stand, split by a vertical ray.
You had better walk with the wave. Walk the wave – don't hurt
    your feet.
In the wave's embrace you never know you are drowning.

5

And then He comes. He lays his yoke
on your back. You feel it, you tremble, you are awake.

Schizoid

There are moments, hollow without hope;
will I ever light up a thought,
ever strike warm sparks from my heart?

Don't push me aside, don't recoil from my anger.
This isn't anger – no, no – it's only an empty shore.

The slightest weight is too much for me,
I walk on and feel I'm not moving at all.

You never stand still, remember; your strength
recharges in silence: it will find its way.
Your strength will explode.

And then without violence, not instantly wholly yourself,
you must give heart-space to your moments, space to the
        pressure of will.

There is growth in hollow stagnation;
your fever-shot eyes must not
burn it to ashes.

The blind man

Tapping the pavement with a white stick
we create the necessary distance.
Each step costs us dear.
In our blank pupils the world dies
unrecognizable to itself:

the world of cracking noise, not colour
(only lines, murmuring outlines).
For us how difficult to become whole,
a part is always left out
and that is the part we have to choose.

How gladly would we take up the weight
of man who seizes space without a white stick.
How will you teach us there are wrongs
besides our own?
Will you convince us there is happiness
in being blind?

Actor

So many grew round me, through me,
from my self, as it were.
I became a channel, unleashing a force
called man.
Did not the others crowding in, distort
the man that I am?
Being each of them, always imperfect,
myself to myself too near,
he who survives in me, can he ever
look at himself without fear?

Girl disappointed in love

With mercury we measure pain
as we measure the heat of bodies and air;
but this is not how to discover our limits –
you think you are the centre of things.
If you could only grasp that you are not:
the centre is He,
and He, too, finds no love –
why don't you see?

The human heart – what is it for?
Cosmic temperature. Heart. Mercury.

Children

Growing unawares through love, of a sudden
they've grown up, and hand in hand
wander in crowds (their hearts caught like birds,
profiles pale in the dusk).
The pulse of mankind beats in their hearts.

On a bank by the river, holding hands –
a tree stump in moonlight, the earth a half-whisper –
the children's hearts rise over the water.
Will they be changed when they get up and go?

Or look at it this way: a goblet of light tilted
over a plant reveals unknown inwardness.
Will you spoil what has begun in you?
Will you always separate the right from the wrong?

The car factory worker

Smart new models from under my fingers:
whirring already in distant streets.
I am not with them at the controls
on sleek motorways; the policeman's in charge.
They stole my voice; it's the cars that speak.

My soul is open: I want to know
with whom I am fighting, for whom I live.
Thoughts stronger than words. No answers.
Such questions mustn't be asked out loud.
Just be back every day at six in the morning.
What makes you think that man
can tip the balance on the scales of the world?

The armaments factory worker

I cannot influence the fate of the globe.
Do I start wars? How can I know
whether I'm for or against?
No, I don't sin.
It worries me not to have influence,
that it is not I who sin.
I only turn screws, weld together
parts of destruction,
never grasping the whole,
or the human lot.

I could do otherwise (would parts be left out?)
contributing then to sanctified toil
which no one would blot out in action
or belie in speech.
Though what I create is all wrong,
the world's evil is none of my doing.

But is that enough?

Magdalene

The spirit has shifted, my body remains
in its old place. Pain overtakes me
to last as long as I grow in my body.
Now I can give it food from the spirit
where before there was only hunger.

At times love aches: there are weeks, months, years.
Like the roots of a dry tree my tongue is dry
and the roof of my mouth. My lips are unpainted.
Truth sounding out error.

But it is He who feels
the drought of the whole world, not I.

Man of emotion

You don't really suffer when love is flooding you:
it's a patch of enthusiasm, pleasant and shallow;
if it dries up – do you think of the void?
Between heart and heart there is always a gap.
You must enter it slowly –
till the eye absorbs colour,
the ear tunes to rhythm.

Love and move inwards, discover your will,
shed heart's evasions and the mind's harsh control.

Man of intellect

Robbing your life of charm and variety,
the taste of adventure, of space, spontaneity.

How cramped are your notions, formulas, judgements,
always condensing yet hungry for content.

Don't break down my defences, accept the human lot;
each road must take the direction of thought.

Man of will

Colourless moment of will yet heavy as piston's drive,
or sharp as a whip,
a moment that, on the whole,
encroaches on nobody –
or only on me.
It doesn't ripen like fruit, out of feeling,
or emerge from thought,
it just shortens the road.
When it comes I must lift it up
and this I do, on the whole.

No place for heart and thought,
only the moment exploding
in me, the cross.

Simon of Cyrene

Eye to eye with this man. The street. Many faces.
Pounding in my temples as in a forge.
Nothing adventurous for me. I don't want to offend;
let me keep myself to myself.
No beggar or convict will ever break into me;
neither will God.

I want to be fair so I bargain with you bullies
over that man
(though I would rather be back in town).
I bargain for justice –
not my lot, rightly, yet grace for him.

But I want to be fair, so I bargain with you bullies.
No, don't go too far, don't touch my thoughts
or my heart – you'll stir nothing there. This rough handling,
this violence – and he dares, he accepts it, a beggar!

Well, a fair man so far – what next?
People will come, women and children, all the same people,
and with him – me.
Who is to say which is which
when the weight knocks us both to the ground –
me and him?
I cannot stand this – justice is not made of steel.

Smash it to pieces, open it up! (Sentences must be compact,
words must speed urgently on, no well-rounded stanzas).
Smash it and open it up.
An eye hangs above me, rays pour from the heart;
higher than the cross-beam,
the eye is so high I can't reach it.

My petty world:
justice squeezed out, rules, regulations.
Your world is so big:
the eye, the cross-beam and he.
You could overlook the pettiness in your great world,
smash my world to nothing;
bearing the cross you could bring it all to the brink.
You are accessible, broad: all men are contained in you.

No, I don't want mere justice now.
I stand on a threshold, glimpse a new world.
A crowd passes by: women, children, soldiers;
they mill round near the frontier with God.
Silence. Silence.
Justice calls for rebellion. But rebellion against whom?

The Church

(The Basilica of St Peter, autumn 1962; 11 October – 8 December)

Wall

A straight wall, a fragment of the wall; I see
the niches, flat pilasters on either side,
with figures of saints stopped as they glide,
and in a single movement show
some vast movement sweeping from
the open books.

And the vaults are no weight to the wall
nor are the living men who inhabit
the single rooms of their tired hearts
far away.

Even the abyss surrounding the earth now
is no burden
while man is born an infant
suckled at his mother's breast.

Abyss

Abyssus abyssum invocat

You always see it as space
filled with cascades of air
where glass splinters reflect and glitter
like seeds planted in distant stones.

Now observe the abyss that glitters
in the eye's reflection.
We all bear it in us.
When men are gathered together
they shift the abyss like a boat
on their shoulders.

Nothing to bypass in this commotion.
Take a ray from the eye and write
your sign.
Though you see no abyss in the mind
don't imagine that it is not there.
Light may not reach your sight, but the boat
shifts on to your shoulders:
the abyss is clothed in flesh,
become fact
in all men.

The Negro

My dear brother, it's you, an immense land I feel
where rivers dry up suddenly – and the sun
burns the body as the foundry burns ore.
I feel your thought like mine;
if they diverge the balance is the same:
in the scales truth and error.
There is joy in weighing thoughts on the same scales,
thoughts that differently flicker in your eyes and mine
though their substance is the same.

Marble floor

Our feet meet the earth in this place;
there are so many walls, so many colonnades,
yet we are not lost. If we find
meaning and oneness,
it is the floor that guides us. It joins the spaces
of this great edifice, and joins
the spaces within us,
who walk aware of our weakness and defeat.
Peter, you are the floor, that others
may walk over you (not knowing
where they go). You guide their steps
so that spaces can be one in their eyes,
and from them thought is born.
You want to serve their feet that pass
as rock serves the hooves of sheep.
The rock is a gigantic temple floor,
the cross a pasture.

The crypt

We must go below the marble floor,
with its generations of footsteps,
and drill through the rock to find the man
trampled by hooves of sheep.
They knew not whom they trampled – a passing man?
the Man who never will pass?
The crypt speaks: I am bound to the world and besieged;
the world is an army of exhausted soldiers
who will not pull back.

Synodus

They all start up again and again:
no graveyard for tiredness; even the very old,
hardly able to move on their knees, are prepared for the stadium.
Eyes both fading and young see what is whole:
the world which must come from their bodies and souls,
from the life that they give and the death they desire.
That world will come like a thief and steal all we possess.
Poor and naked, we will be transparent as glass
that both cuts and reflects.
Lashed by conscience, this vast temple its setting,
the split world must grow whole.

Gospel

Truth doesn't drip oil into wounds to stop the burning pain,
or sit you on a donkey to be led through the streets;
truth must be hurtful and hide.
Structures contract in the brain: raised in man
a building leans; we want to straighten
not its pediment but the ground resisting far beneath
as waves resist boats.

Truth supports man. When he can't lift himself,
indeed the building weighs double.
We all find it in us, a mysterious mould;
we range over astounded streets
where the donkey is led.
(Is there less and less truth in the streets – or more?)
We look ahead calmly: we are beyond dread.

Springs and hands

We have words to lean on, spoken long ago,
still spoken in trembling for fear they should change.
But is this all?

For there are invisible hands that hold us
so that it takes great effort to carry the boat,
whose story, despite the shallows, follows its course.

Is it enough to dip deep in the spring,
not to seek the invisible hands?

Two cities
(epilogue)

Each of the two cities is a whole,
which cannot be carried from heart to heart;
each has to live at our heart's expense,
in each – each of us.

Unless we are wholly at one with one of the two,
we cannot exist and remain true.
(Long hours we talk of this
above the lights of the Third City,
at its best self in the evening
when the day's tinsel is cast off.)

The Birth of Confessors

I. A bishop's thoughts on giving the sacrament of confirmation in a mountain village

1

The world is charged with hidden energies
and boldly I call them by name.
No flat words; though ready to leap
they don't hurtle like mountain water on stones
or flash past like trees from sight.

Take a good look at them as you would
watch insects through a windowpane.
And still, and yet – under the words' surface
feel the ground, how firm to your feet.
(This thought is composed of currents,
not of innumerable drops).

I am a giver, I touch forces that expand the mind;
sometimes the memory of a starless night
is all that remains.

2

Inward-bent, so many they are, they stand in slanting files.
A frail flower, it seems, sprouts from the street
to take root in their hearts.

3

In their features I see a field, even and white,
upturned, their temples a slope,
their eyebrows a line below.
The touch of my open hand
senses the trust.

Thought is behind it, a thought – not seeing
but choosing. In the map of their wrinkles
is there the will to fight?
Shadow moves over their faces.
An electric field vibrates.

4

Electricity is fact not symbol.
I look through eyelashes into the eyes:
light through a transparent grove.

The surface connects with the hidden plane,
a frontier running untouched by sight;
thoughts rise to the eyes like moths to the pane,
they silently shine in the pupils – deep,
how deep are human deeds.

5

We never see spirit – eye mirrors thought;
I meet thought half way and then turn back.
The eye competes with the face,
opening it up, wiping its shadows away.

6

The shape of the face says everything
(where else such expression of being?).
How telling the eyes of a child,
constantly crossing a strange equator
(the earth remains a small atom of thought).

Invisible pressures are trapped in the atmosphere,
yet there is light enough
to approach in this dark.

7

And who is to come?

8

Everything else enclosed in itself:
grass on the crest of the wind,
an apple tree cradled in space
abundant with fruit.
Man meets Him who walks always ahead,
courage their meeting place,
each man a fortress.

II. Thoughts of a man receiving the sacrament of confirmation in a mountain village

1

How am I to be born?
Will I go with the light that flows
like a mountain stream,
saying: dry, dry, dry is the river bed,
then, suddenly, stumble
like a child on a taut rope,
stumble over a thought, a threshold,
the water beating my heart and taking my peace away.

Must I ask for a spring? Is it enough to walk
with the stream, never stop, never counter a wave –

And to counter – is it to confess?
Thought perhaps must first be formed, toil born
(like opening a gate against the tide,
mooring the boat to a slender stake).

2

Must my thought occupy everything, on, on to the end?
May I never think for myself, for my own sake?
Never think of myself as a *curious phenomenon*,
always recall that I am but a *casual existence*?

3

If I have truth in me, it will break out one day.
I cannot repel it: my own self I'd repel.

4

(Thoughts about a foot-bridge)

I take my first steps on a foot-bridge.
My heart – is it a foot-bridge throbbing in each joist?
Is thought a foot-bridge?
(My thoughts only trace what my heart is tracking.
Feelings, perceptions – but which fill me more?)
This foot-bridge is all.
And yet I grow differently,
feel the wind differently, differently sway.
Both strong and weak speak to me
and strength is the contrast:
the world leans differently
on strength and on weakness.

Is the bridge just an image of somebody crossing?
Over the deep, groping for the shore, he throbs
at the merging of currents.

In himself man feels no weight of hours:
they hang overhead, and they vanish below.

5

And yet I stand,
a profile cut from the wave
which withdraws and leaves me behind.
My motion is other:
there a shape is enclosed in transparent brackets,
here the truth is confirmed
in my own life.

6

Wait. Have patience. I will draw You
from all river-beds, streams, springs of light,
from the roots of trees and the plains of the sun.
When all this is in me,
when I contain the dual weight of terror and hope
and reach depths translucent as sky.
then no one will say
that I simplify.

A conversation with God begins

The human body in history dies more often and earlier
than the tree.
Man endures beyond the doors of death in catacombs and crypts.
Man who departs endures in those who follow.
Man who follows endures in those departed.
Man endures beyond all coming and going
in himself
and in you.

The history of men, such as I, always looks for the body
you will give them.
Each man in history loses his body and goes towards you.
In the moment of departure
each is greater than history
although but a part
(a fragment of a century or two,
merged into one life).

A conversation with man begins: the meaning of things

On this point we cannot agree.
He says: man is condemned only to loss
of his body. Man's history seeks nothing
but the body of things: these remain
while man dies
and generations live on them.
But things don't die a personal death,
man is left with the immortality of things.

This I say: much of man dies in things,
more than remains. Have you tried to embrace
what does not die and find for it
profile and space?
Don't speak of unknowns.
Man is not an unknown.
Man is always made human.
Never separate man from things, the body
of his history. Never separate people from Man who became
the body of their history. Things cannot save
what is utterly human – only Man.

We stand in front of our future
which closes and opens at the same time.
Do not close the oneness of comings and goings
with wilful abstraction:
life throbbed and blood dripped in them.
Return to each place where a man died; return to the place
where he was born. The past is the time of birth, not of death.

Invocation to Man who became the body of history

I call you and I seek you, in whom
man's history finds its body.
I go towards you and do not say 'come'
but simply 'be'.

Be where there is no record, yet where man was,
was with his soul, his heart, desire, suffering and will,
consumed by feeling, burnt by most holy shame.
Be an eternal seismograph of the invisible but real.

Oh, Man, in whom our lowest depths meet our heights,
for whom what is within is not a dark burden but the heart.
Man in whom each man can find his deep design,
and the roots of his deeds: the mirror of life and death
staring at the human flux.

Through the shallows of history I always reach you
walking towards each heart, walking towards each thought
(history – the overcrowding of thoughts, death of hearts).
I seek your body for all history,
I seek your depth.

Właściwa inwokacja czyli wołanie do człowieka, który stał się ciałem historii

Do Ciebie wołam, Człowieku, Ciebie szukam – w którym
historia ludzi może znaleźć swe Ciało.
Ku Tobie idę, i nie mówię ,,przybądź",
ale po prostu ,,bądź",

bądź tam, gdzie w rzeczach żaden nie widnieje zapis, a człowiek
był,
był duszą, sercem, pragnieniem, cierpieniem i wolą,
gdzie go trawiły uczucia i palił najświętszy wstyd –
bądź jak wieczysty Sejsmograf tego, co niewidzialne a
Rzeczywiste.
Człowieku, w którym ludzkie dno się spotyka i ludzki szczyt,
w którym wnętrze nie jest ciężarem i mrokiem, lecz właśnie
sercem.

Człowieku, w którym każdy człowiek odnaleźć może zamysł
najgłębszy
i korzeń własnych uczynków: zwierciadło życia i śmierci
wpatrzone w ludzki nurt.
Do Ciebie – Człowieku – stale docieram przez płytką rzekę
historii,
idąc w stronę serca każdego, idąc w stronę każdej myśli
(historia – myśli stłoczeniem i śmiercią serc).
Szukam dla całej historii Twojego Ciała,
szukam Twej głębi.

(*Invocation to Man* . . . in the Polish original)

61

Notes

The original texts of the poems translated here from Polish appeared between 1950 and 1966 in two Catholic periodicals: *Tygodnik Powszechny* (abbreviated as *TP*) and *Znak*, both published in Cracow.

from MOTHER (*Matka*, published in *TP*, 10 December 1950), a group of eight poems, of which three are translated:
Her amazement at her only child (*Zdumienie nad Jednorodzonym*)
John beseeches her (*Prośba Jana*)
Embraced by new time (*Objęta nowym czasem*)

from SONG OF THE BRIGHTNESS OF WATER (*Pieśń o blasku wody*, published in *TP*, 7 May 1950), a group of eight poems, of which five are translated:
Looking into the well at Sichar (*Nad studnią w Sychem*)
Words spoken by the woman at the well, on departing (*Słowa niewiasty u studni, które wypowiedziała odchodząc*)
The Samaritan woman (*Samarytanka*)
The Samaritan woman meditates (*Rozważania ponowne*)
Song of the brightness of water (*Pieśń o blasku wody*)

from THOUGHT – STRANGE SPACE (*Myśl jest przestrzenią dziwną*, published in *TP*, 19 October 1952), a group of eight poems, of which three are translated:
Thought's resistance to words (*Opór stawiany wyrazom przez myśli*)
Words' resistance to thought (*Opór stawiany myślom przez wyrazy*)
Error (*Błąd*)

THE QUARRY (*Kamieniołom*, published in *Znak*, November 1957), a poem in four parts, written in 1956:
 I. Material (*Tworzywo*)
 II. Inspiration (*Natchnienie*)
 III. Participation (*Uczestnictwo*)
 IV. (In memory of a fellow-worker) (*Pamięci towarzysza pracy*)

from PROFILES OF A CYRENEAN (*Profile Cyrenejczyka*, published in *TP*, 23 March 1958), written in 1957, a cycle of sixteen poems, of which thirteen are translated:
 Before I could discern many profiles (*Zanim jeszcze potrafiłem rozróżnić wiele profilów*)
 Schizoid (*Schizotymik* – the Polish title refers to a term in Ernst Kretschmer's typology, denoting a person immersed in himself and isolated)
 The blind man (*Niewidomi*)
 Actor (*Aktor*)
 Girl disappointed in love (*Dziewczyna zawiedziona w miłości*)
 Children (*Dzieci*)
 The car factory worker (*Robotnik z fabryki samochodów*)
 The armaments factory worker (*Robotnik z fabryki broni*)
 Magdalene (*Magdalena*)
 Man of emotion (*Człowiek emocji*)
 Man of intellect (*Człowiek intelektu*)
 Man of will (*Człowiek woli*)
 Simon of Cyrene (*Szymon z Cyreny*)

THE CHURCH (*Kościół*, published in *Znak*, November 1963) also has a subtitle, 'Shepherds and Springs' (*Pasterze i źródła*). A sequence of nine poems:
 Wall (*Ściana*)
 Abyss (*Przepaść*)

The Negro (*Murzyn*), addressed to one of the African bishops
    attending the Vatican Council
Marble floor (*Posadzka*)
The crypt (*Krypta*)
Synodus (*Synodus*)
Gospel (*Ewangelia*)
Springs and hands (*Źródła i ręce*)
Two cities (*Dwa miasta*)

THE BIRTH OF CONFESSORS (*Narodziny wyznawców*), two
poems written in 1961, which follow 'Shepherds and Springs' in
THE CHURCH (above).
  I. A bishop's thoughts on giving the sacrament of
    confirmation in a mountain village (*Myśli biskupa
    udzielającego sakramentu bierzmowania w pewnej podgórskiej
    wsi*)
  II. Thoughts of a man receiving the sacrament of confirmation
    in a mountain village (*Myśli człowieka przyjmującego
    sakrament bierzmowania w pewnej podgórskiej wsi*)

from EASTER VIGIL 1966 (*Wigilia wielkanocna 1966*, published
in *Znak*, April 1966), a sequence in seven parts, inspired by
Poland's thousand years as a Christian state. Three poems from
the part 'Invocation' (*Inwokacja*) are translated:
    A conversation with God begins (*Rozpoczyna się rozmowa z
    Bogiem*)
    A conversation with man begins: the meaning of things
    (*Rozpoczyna się rozmowa z człowiekiem, spór o znaczenie
    rzeczy*)
    Invocation to Man who became the body of history
    (*Właściwa inwokacja czyli wołanie do człowieka, który stał się
    ciałem historii*)

64

Leabharlanna Atha Cliath